Festivals in Different Cultures

Chinese New Year

by Lisa J. Amstutz

raintree

a Capstone company — publishers for children

Raintree is an imprint of Capstone Global Library Limited, a company incorporated in England and Wales having its registered office at 264 Banbury Road, Oxford, OX2 7DY – Registered company number: 6695582

www.raintree.co.uk
myorders@raintree.co.uk

Text © Capstone Global Library Limited 2017
The moral rights of the proprietor have been asserted.

Edited by Jill Kalz
Designed by Julie Peters
Picture research by Pam Mitsakos
Production by Steve Walker

Printed and bound in India.

ISBN 978 1 4747 3791 3 (hardback)
20 19 18 17 16
10 9 8 7 6 5 4 3 2 1

ISBN 978 1 4747 3797 5 (paperback)
21 20 19 18 17
10 9 8 7 6 5 4 3 2 1

British Library Cataloguing in Publication Data
A full catalogue record for this book is available from the British Library.

Acknowledgements
We would like to thank the following for permission to reproduce photographs: Getty Images: MIXA, 9, View Stock, 11; iStockphoto: FangXiaNuo, 6, IS_ImageSource, 15; Shutterstock: 123Nelson, 21, asharkyu, cover, freelion, 7, iBird, 5, macbrianmun, 10, maoyunping, 1, passion artist, design element, Sofiaworld, 3 bottom left, Tan Kian Khoon, 20 bottom right, Toa55, back cover, topten22photo, 19; Superstock: Blue Jean Images, 17, Neil Farrin /robertharding, 13

Every effort has been made to contact copyright holders of material reproduced in this book. Any omissions will be rectified in subsequent printings if notice is given to the publisher.

All the Internet addresses (URLs) given in this book were valid at the time of going to press. However, due to the dynamic nature of the Internet, some addresses may have changed, or sites may have changed or ceased to exist since publication. While the author and publisher regret any inconvenience this may cause readers, no responsibility for any such changes can be accepted by either the author or the publisher.

Contents

Happy New Year!

Pop! Boom!

Fireworks fill the sky.

It is Chinese New Year!

This holiday is in January or February. It lasts many days.

Let's get ready

People clean their homes.

They sweep out bad luck.

9

People hang red scrolls.

Red is a lucky colour.

Many people shop for gifts. They buy flowers. They get new clothes.

Time for a party

It is New Year's Eve!

Families gather.

They eat a big meal.

The next day, kids get red envelopes. Money is inside. Friends visit. They bring wishes for good luck.

The holiday ends with
a parade. Lanterns glow.
People eat sweets.
They beat drums.

Dancers dress up as lions. A dragon runs by. People cheer. Happy New Year!

Glossary

envelope flat, folded paper

fireworks rockets that make loud noises and colourful lights when they explode

lantern container for a light

parade line of people, bands and floats that travels through a town for a special event

scroll roll of paper with writing on it

Read more

Chinese New Year (Holidays and Festivals),
Nancy Dickman (Raintree, 2011)

Chinese New Year (Festivals Around the World),
Grace Jones (BookLife, 2015)

Chinese New Year (Sparklers - Celebrations),
Katie Dickers (Laburnum Press, 2013)

Websites

www.topmarks.co.uk/ChineseNewYear/ChineseNewYear.aspx
Discover what Chinese New Year is all about. Play a Chinese Dragon game or make a Happy New Year card!

www.timeanddate.com/holidays/uk/chinese-new-year
Learn how the Chinese New Year is celebrated in the UK.

Comprehension questions

1. How do people get ready for Chinese New Year?
2. Name three red things that may be seen during Chinese New Year.

Index